Parrots
of the
Caribbean

Steve Barlow and Steve Skidmore
Illustrated by Jez Tuya

Pirate Warrrrning ...

This is the story of the wickedest pirates that ever sailed the Caribbean Sea. This book is NOT for chicken-hearted landlubbers. If you're the sort of person who faints at the sight of blood, do NOT read this book ...

You have been warrrned, matey!

Oooh-arrrrrr!

Chapter 1
All at sea

Captain Cut-Throat's black beard bristled with anger. 'You, matey, are the worst pirate I have ever seen.'

Doghouse Dave backed away from the Captain's angry face and bad breath. 'I'm very sorry, sir,' he stammered.

'"Sorry" isn't good enough!' roared Captain Cut-Throat. He waved a crumpled map under Doghouse Dave's nose. 'What's the meaning of this?'

Doghouse Dave gulped. 'Well, Captain, you told me to draw a map of the island where you buried your treasure ... '

'Aye, you fish-headed fool!'

'And you told me to put an X where the treasure was. Well, I was drawing the map and I started thinking about Fishbone Sal – she's the girl of my dreams – and I never noticed I was drawing little kisses all over the map ... '

'I can see that!' Captain Cut-Throat held up the map, which was covered in tiny crosses. 'Five hundred 'X's mark the spot! But which one is my treasure buried under?'

Doghouse Dave whimpered, 'I can't remember ... '

'You pudding-head! I'll have to dig the whole island up to find it again! I've a good mind to feed you to the sharks!'

'Please, sir,' begged Doghouse Dave. 'Give me another chance!'

The Captain grinned a wicked grin. 'All right then. There's a leak below decks.' He gave Doghouse Dave a kick in the seat of his pants. 'Get down there and fix it! And don't come back up here until you have, or else!'

Doghouse Dave went down to the bottom of the ship. The water was sloshing around his knees. It would take ages to find the leak that was letting the water in ...

Unless, of course, he first let the water that was already in, *out*. A cunning smile spread over Doghouse Dave's face.

Five minutes later, he had fetched a drill from the carpenter's store. Chuckling at his own cleverness, Doghouse Dave began to make a hole in the very bottom of the ship. He'd have this leak fixed in no time!

Chapter 2
Marooned!

Doghouse Dave watched sadly as *The Pirate Queen* sailed away. Captain Cut-Throat's distant voice called, 'Watch out for cannibals and crocodiles, matey! Ha ha! Ooo-arr!' Then the ship was gone.

Doghouse Dave couldn't blame the Captain. His hole hadn't let water *out*, it had let more water *in*. He'd almost sunk the ship.

Now he was marooned on a desert island with nothing but a knife, a bottle of water and half a ship's biscuit.

'What am I going to do now?' he moaned.

'Search me,' said a voice.

Doghouse Dave spun round quickly. 'Who said that?'

'I did.' A parrot flew down from a nearby tree. 'Hello,' he said. 'My name is JoJo.'

'Are you a pirate's parrot?' asked Doghouse Dave.

'What makes you say that?' said JoJo.

'It's the headscarf. And the earring. And the wooden leg.'

'Yeah,' said JoJo, 'those are a bit of a give-away I suppose. I was a pirate's parrot. I belonged to Short John Silver. When we were marooned here, he went mad and swam out to sea. The only problem was he couldn't swim.'

Doghouse Dave sighed. 'I think I'll go mad, too, if I have to stay here.'

'Why don't you escape, then?' said JoJo.

'How?'

'Good grief,' said JoJo. 'How stupid are humans? What you need is a signal, so a passing ship will know you're here. Start a fire or something.'

'I don't know how to start a fire,' said Doghouse Dave.

'But I do,' said JoJo. 'You have to rub two sticks together. I made one once with Short John's wooden leg. The only problem was he forgot to take it off first. I nearly burnt him to the ground!'

In no time at all, the fire was crackling away.

Dave smiled. 'It's a shame we haven't got a kettle. I could have said, "Polly put the kettle on"!'

JoJo shook his head. 'Not funny, Dave. Not funny.'

A few hours later, a ship appeared on the horizon. Doghouse Dave danced for joy. 'We're saved!' he cried.

But JoJo let out a squawk of terror. 'That's what you think! That ship looks like the *Saucy Poll*. Its crew is the worst collection of thieves and villains on the Spanish Main. Haven't you ever heard of … the Parrots of the Caribbean?'

Chapter 3

Captain Kid

The rowing boat from the *Saucy Poll* landed on the beach.

'Let me do the talking,' whispered JoJo. 'I'm the wordy birdie.'

Three miserable-looking pirates got out. Each had a parrot on his shoulder. All the parrots had headscarves and earrings.

JoJo flapped a wing to greet them. 'Ahoy, shipmates! I'm JoJo and this is my stupid human.'

One of the pirates held out his hand to
Doghouse Dave. 'I'm Numbskull Ned – Ow!'
he screeched, as the parrot on his shoulder bit
his ear.

'No-one cares who you are!' snapped the
parrot. It turned to JoJo. 'Ahoy, matey. I'm
KiKi. This is Olly and that is Jeff. Is there any
fruit on this island?'

'Sure is. I'll show you.' JoJo and the other
parrots flew off towards the trees.

Doghouse Dave stared at Numbskull Ned's bleeding ear. 'Why did your parrot do that?'

'Oh, those parrots are always a-pecking and a-biting if we talk without permission,' moaned Numbskull Ned. 'Ask Bonehead Basil. He'll tell you.'

'Aye,' said the second pirate. 'Ask Clueless Charlie. He'll tell you.'

Clueless Charlie scratched his head. 'Tell him what?'

'Look out!' said Doghouse Dave. 'They're coming back!'

'Sshh,' said Numbskull Ned.

'Right, everyone back in the boat,' ordered KiKi. 'It's time to meet the Captain.'

The pirates stayed silent as they rowed back to their ship. They pushed Doghouse Dave up the *Saucy Poll*'s side and he tumbled onto the deck.

'Look lively!' JoJo whispered in Dave's ear. 'Bow to Captain Kid!'

Doghouse Dave looked up into the eyes of a very small pirate. He was wearing a captain's uniform. 'Captain Kid?' Dave blurted. 'But he's ... he's ... '

The parrot on the Captain's shoulder gave him an angry look. 'He's what, you scurvy swab?'

Doghouse Dave giggled. 'He's just a kid!'

JoJo closed his eyes. 'Now you've done it!'

The Captain's parrot flapped its wings and screeched, 'Mutiny!'

Chapter 4
Doghouse Dave's brainwave

'We're in big trouble now, matey,' said JoJo.

'Really?' Doghouse Dave rattled his chains. 'What makes you think that?'

They were lying in the deepest, darkest part of the ship, with only the rats for company.

'They'll probably make us walk the plank in the morning,' said JoJo.

'Well, you'll be all right. When you get to the end of the plank you can just fly off.'

'Not in these chains, I can't! I'm going to be a dead parrot.'

Doghouse Dave laughed. 'Then you'll be a polygon. Geddit? Polly-gone!'

JoJo shook his head. 'Not funny, Dave. Not funny.'

A light appeared through the gloom. It was Captain Kid, holding a lantern.

'Hello,' he whispered. 'Please don't make a noise – MacAw would be very cross if he knew I was here.'

Doghouse Dave thought for a moment. 'MacAw? Is he your parrot?'

Captain Kid nodded. 'Yes. He's very bad-tempered. He bosses me around. I'm only a cabin boy really.'

'Oh,' said Dave. 'I thought you were the Captain!'

'MacAw made the other pirates choose me,' said Captain Kid. 'They're all terrified of their parrots, and all the other parrots are terrified of MacAw. He'd probably bite my ear right off if he knew I was talking to you.'

'Then why are you here?' squawked JoJo.

'I just wanted to say sorry for sending you down here – and for putting you in chains. It was MacAw's idea.'

'Where's MacAw now?' asked Doghouse Dave.

'He's snoring on his perch,' said Captain Kid. 'So are all the other parrots.'

'Couldn't you just let us go while they're asleep?' said Doghouse Dave hopefully.

Captain Kid shook his head. 'They'd peck us all to bits when they found out.' He scratched his head. 'If only there was some way we could get rid of them for good!'

Doghouse Dave's face lit up. 'I've got an idea!'

'Captain, do you have any treasure on board?' asked Dave.

'Yes, we have lots of treasure,' said Captain Kid sadly. 'The parrots keep making us sink other ships. They're very greedy.'

'So you have gold and silver?' said Dave.

'Yes, tons of it,' replied Captain Kid.

'And metal polish?' said Dave.

'Yes.' Captain Kid looked puzzled. 'Why?'

'I'll explain later,' Doghouse Dave said firmly. 'Now let us out of these chains and then call your men. We've got work to do ... '

Chapter 5

Pirates and parrots part

When the parrots woke up at dawn, they came out on deck. They found lots of gold and silver bowls and plates hanging in the ship's rigging.

'What's all this?' squawked MacAw angrily. Then he caught sight of his reflection in a golden bowl. His eyes opened wide. 'Oh,' he simpered. 'Who's a pretty birdie?'

Soon, all the parrots were staring at the pieces of treasure that the pirates had spent all night polishing. Cries of 'Who's a pretty birdie, then?' echoed from every part of the ship.

'So that was your plan!' cried Captain Kid. 'Those polished plates and bowls are like mirrors!'

Doghouse Dave pointed out to sea. 'There's an island. Now's our chance to escape while they're not looking!' he said.

JoJo was staring at his own reflection with a silly grin on his beak.

'Hey, JoJo!' said Doghouse Dave. 'Are you coming or staying?'

'What?' replied JoJo. 'Oh, I'm coming with you, but I might need some help. I can't take my eyes off this gorgeous parrot here!'

'That's you, you barmy bird!'

'Really?' said JoJo. 'Now that *is* funny, Dave.'

The pirates launched the *Saucy Poll*'s rowing boat and headed towards the island. They gathered on the shore as the *Saucy Poll* disappeared from sight.

'Let's hope those pesky parrots don't come looking for us,' said Captain Kid.

JoJo shook his head. 'How are they going to steer the ship without you humans to help them? You're safe, matey!'

The pirates danced for joy. 'We're free! Hurrah!'

As Doghouse Dave had turned out to be quite clever after all, the pirates made him their new captain. They decided to give up piracy altogether and live on the island. They lay in the sun eating fruit and coconuts, and Dave spent his days dreaming of Fishbone Sal.

As for the Parrots of the Caribbean, they drifted away across the mighty ocean.

And for all we know, they may well be drifting there still ...

CN 3/14

About the authors

Ahoy there, me hearties! Steve 'Greybeard' Barlow and Steve 'Pegleg' Skidmore have been sailing the high seas of writing for over twenty years. They've plundered stories for over 175 books. They are one of the UK's most popular writing and performing double acts for young cut-throats who like comedy and adventure.

They love tales about pirates ... and parrots.

Ooo-arr!